Succeeding with the Masters
& The Festival Collection®
ETUDES with Technique

About the Series

This series is designed to develop healthy, natural, and effective technique so students can play beautifully as well as with virtuosity. Each book is divided into units, and each unit focuses on one technical concept. Technical concepts are introduced using imagery to help the student understand the gesture needed to produce the correct technique. Different imagery is used in each level of this series. Following the text and the imagery, two short technical exercises provide the student's first opportunity to play the technique. These exercises should be memorized so students can focus on the sound they produce while observing their playing mechanism in action. Several etudes then follow to reinforce each technical concept. In this way, students focus on one technique at a time, and the concept is reinforced through multiple etudes. This method allows the student to master the technique and make it a habit, providing the foundation for effective, natural, relaxed, and enjoyable performances of their repertoire.

The student should concentrate on looking at their hands and being aware of the feeling in their fingers and fingertips, hands, wrists, forearms, elbows, and upper arms so as to produce the correct gestures. To achieve a fluid and solid technique, students must always listen carefully to themselves and the sound they create.

This series is best used with the following publications:

Etudes with Technique, Book 1 = The Festival Collection®, Book 1 = On Your Way to Succeeding with the Masters®
Etudes with Technique, Book 2 = The Festival Collection®, Book 2 = An Introduction to Succeeding with the Masters® =
Succeeding with the Masters®, Volume One
Etudes with Technique, Book 3 = The Festival Collection®, Book 3 = Succeeding with the Masters®, Volume One
Etudes with Technique, Book 4 = The Festival Collection®, Book 4 = Succeeding with the Masters®, Volume One

Production: Frank J. Hackinson
Production Coordinators: Joyce Loke and Satish Bhakta
Cover Art Concept: Helen Marlais
Cover Design: Terpstra Design, San Francisco, CA
Illustration: Keith Criss, TradigitalWorks, Oakland, CA
Engraving: Tempo Music Press, Inc.
Printer: Tempo Music Press, Inc.

ISBN-13: 978-1-61928-021-2

Etudes with Technique, Book 4

Unit	Composer	Title	Page
1		**Five-Finger Patterns and Extensions**	8
	Loeschhorn, Albert	Etude (*Op. 65, No. 7*)	9
	Le Couppey, Félix	Etude (*Op. 17, No. 2*)	10
	Roubos, Valerie Roth	Running Late	11
	Stravinsky, Soulima	Tag, from *Children's Pieces, No. 8*	12
	Hassler, Hans Leo	Etude (*Op. 38, No. 19*)	13
2		**Triads and Inversions**	14
	Köhler, Louis	Etude (*Op. 300, No. 75*)	15
	Köhler, Louis	Christmas Bells (*Op. 210, No. 25*)	16
	Gurlitt, Cornelius	The Return (*Op. 117, No. 24*)	18
	Czerny, Carl	Etude No. 21, from *One Hundred Recreations*	19
	Schultz, Robert	Wind Master	20
3		**Scale Preparation and Octave Scales**	22
	Gurlitt, Cornelius	Etude (*Op. 82, No. 34*)	23
	Gurlitt, Cornelius	Etude (*Op. 117, No. 12*)	24
	Brown, Timothy	Etude in C *Study in Scales*	25
	Biehl, Albert	Etude (*Op. 44, No. 8*)	26
	Beyer, Ferdinand	Etude (*Op. 101, No. 82*)	28
	Berens, Hermann	Etude (*Op. 70, No. 33*)	29

FJH2028

Unit	Composer	Title	Page
4		**Slurs and Phrasing**	30
	Bertini, Henri	Etude *(Op. 166, No. 12)*	31
	Schytte, Ludwig	Etude *(Op. 108, No. 5)*	32
	Matthay, Tobias/ Swinstead, Felix	Etude No. 5, from *The Pianist's First Music Making*	33
	Roubos, Valerie Roth	Caribbean Sun	34
5		**Broken Chords and Alberti Bass**	36
	Schytte, Ludwig	Etude *(Op. 108, No. 8)*	37
	Croisez, Alexandre	Impatience *(Op. 100, No. 23)*	38
	Bach, Johann Christian/ Ricci, Francesco Pasquale	Etude No. 58, from *Piano Method*	40
6		**Double Notes**	42
	Bartók, Béla	Minuet No. 11, from *First Term at the Piano*	43
	Czerny, Carl	Etude *(Op. 139, No. 7)*	44
	Türk, Daniel Gottlob	For Practicing Thirds and Sixths	45
7		**Repeated Notes**	46
	Schytte, Ludwig	Etude *(Op. 108, No. 10)*	47
	Beyer, Ferdinand	Etude *(Op. 101, No. 90)*	48
	Schultz, Robert	Pranks	49
	Gurlitt, Cornelius	Ringeltanz (Round-dance) *(Op. 74, No. 17)*	50
	Brown, Timothy	Etude in D Minor	52
		About the Pieces and the Composers	53–56

Etudes with Technique, Book 4

Composer	Title	Theme	Page
Bach, Johann Christian / Ricci, Francesco Pasquale	Etude No. 58 from *Piano Method*	*Allegro non troppo*	40
Bartók, Béla	Minuet No. 11 from *First Term at the Piano*	*Andante*	43
Berens, Hermann	Etude (*Op. 70, No. 33*)	*Allegro moderato*	29
Bertini, Henri	Etude (*Op. 166, No. 12*)	*Andante*	31
Beyer, Ferdinand	Etude (*Op. 101, No. 82*)	*Allegretto*	28
Beyer, Ferdinand	Etude (*Op. 101, No. 90*)	*Allegretto*	48
Biehl, Albert	Etude (*Op. 44, No. 8*)	*Un poco allegretto*	26
Brown, Timothy	Etude in C *Study in Scales*	*Allegro*	25
Brown, Timothy	Etude in D Minor	*Andante*	52

Composer	Title	Theme	Page

Croisez, Alexandre . . . . Impatience (*Op. 100, No. 23*) 38

Czerny, Carl . . . . Etude No. 21 19
from *One Hundred Recreations*

Czerny, Carl . . . . Etude (*Op. 139, No. 7*) 44

Gurlitt, Cornelius . . . . Etude (*Op. 82, No. 34*) 23

Gurlitt, Cornelius . . . . Etude (*Op. 117, No. 12*) 24

Gurlitt, Cornelius . . . . Ringeltanz (*Op. 74, No. 17*) 50
(Round-dance)

Gurlitt, Cornelius . . . . The Return (*Op. 117, No. 24*) 18

Hassler, Hans Leo . . . . Etude (*Op. 38, No. 19*) 13

Köhler, Louis . . . . Christmas Bells 16
(*Op. 210, No. 25*)

Composer	Title	Theme	Page
Köhler, Louis	Etude *(Op. 300, No. 75)*		15
Le Couppey, Félix	Etude *(Op. 17, No. 2)*		10
Loeschhorn, Albert	Etude *(Op. 65, No. 7)*		9
Matthay, Tobias/ Swinstead, Felix	Etude No. 5 from *The Pianist's First Music Making*		33
Ricci, Francesco Pasquale/ Bach, Johann Christian	Etude No. 58 from *Piano Method*		40
Roubos, Valerie Roth	Caribbean Sun		34
Roubos, Valerie Roth	Running Late		11
Schultz, Robert	Pranks		49
Schultz, Robert	Wind Master		20

Composer	Title	Theme	Page
Schytte, Ludwig	Etude *(Op. 108, No. 5)*		32
Schytte, Ludwig	Etude *(Op. 108, No. 8)*		37
Schytte, Ludwig	Etude *(Op. 108, No. 10)*		47
Stravinsky, Soulima	Tag from *Children's Pieces, No. 8*		12
Swinstead, Felix / Matthay, Tobias	Etude No. 5 from *The Pianist's First Music Making*		33
Türk, Daniel Gottlob	For Practicing Thirds and Sixths		45

FJH2028

Unit 1 — Five-Finger Patterns and Extensions

You will continue to find five-finger patterns in the music you play, but as the level of difficulty advances, you will be expected to be able to play them quickly and to extend beyond five notes by including wider intervals or crossing the thumb under other fingers. Remember that an even transfer of weight combined with well-timed fingers means you can play with speed and agility. Even as you shift the thumb under to a new location or pass over the thumb to play longer patterns, keep the sweep of the arm much like the motion you might use if you were sanding a long piece of wood. Just as an uneven weight would produce bumps in your smooth finish, a change of weight when crossing the thumb produces bumps in your smooth passagework. Take the time to play the patterns hands separately, using your ear to check that you hear a smooth line and even tone.

Shimmering Pool

Suzanne Torkelson

Transpose to: CM _____

FM _____

Etude

(Opus 65, No. 7)

Albert Loeschhorn
(1819-1905)

• Bring out the left-hand melody.

Etude

(Opus 17, No. 2)

Félix Le Couppey
(1811-1887)

• Listen for the eveness of the L.H. and the articulated two-note slur in the R.H.

RUNNING LATE

Valerie Roth Roubos
(1955-   )

• Listen for the balance between the hands. Which hand will be louder?

TAG

from *Children's Pieces, No. 8*

Soulima Stravinsky
(1910-1994)

• Play with rhythmic precision, not too fast.

Etude

(Opus 38, No. 19)

Hans Leo Hassler
(1564-1612)

• Listen for even and well-shaped scales.

UNIT 2 — TRIADS AND INVERSIONS

Building a secure technique also includes skill in playing three-note triads and their inversions. Think of the solid base of table legs that supports its top—your fingers need to support your rested arm, never collapsing or losing their shape. Check the bridge of your knuckles too; are they the highest part of the hand? The following exercise will help you practice triads and inversions in a "grand" style. Playing broken chords (three or more notes) can always be practiced by blocking them to improve your quick recognition of the notes. Even in pieces that don't appear to have chords, look for skips that build triads to speed up your note learning.

ACCOMPLISHING A GREAT TASK

Helen Marlais

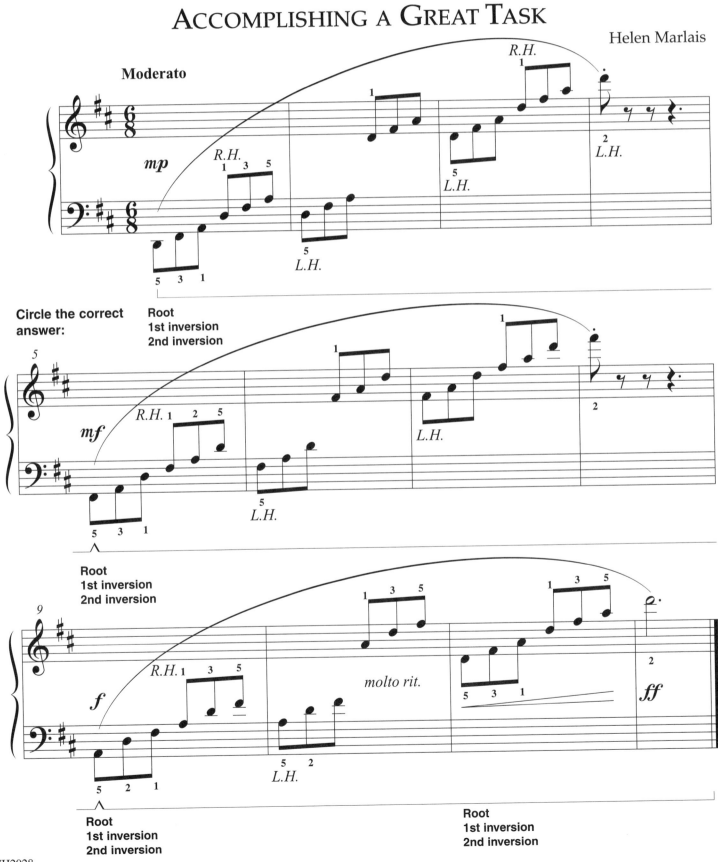

Etude

(Opus 300, No. 75)

Louis Köhler
(1820-1886)

- Play a C Major triad and its inversions, blocked. You can find all of these in this etude.
- Be sure to bring out with expression the hand that plays the melody.

CHRISTMAS BELLS

(Opus 210, No. 25)

Louis Köhler
(1820-1886)

THE RETURN

(Opus 117, No. 24)

Cornelius Gurlitt
(1820 -1901)

- Shift your weight with each triad so that your arm
  supports and is aligned with your hand.

Etude No. 21

from *One Hundred Recreations*

Carl Czerny
(1791-1857)

- Decide which chords in the L.H. are in root position and which ones are played inverted (1st or 2nd inversion).

WIND MASTER

Robert Schultz
(1948 -   )

UNIT 3 — SCALE PREPARATION AND OCTAVE SCALES

Now that you have mastered thumb crossings, you will be able to play scales with evenness and speed. As you try the following exercise, alternate the suggested fingering with occasionally playing fingers 1 through 5. Does it sound the same? When playing scales, "sweep" your arm in the same motion you might use when brushing dust off a flat surface, and you will find that the gesture provides the motion needed to prevent bumps and delays.

SCAMPERING SQUIRRELS

Helen Marlais

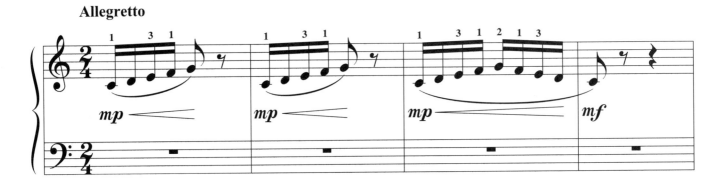

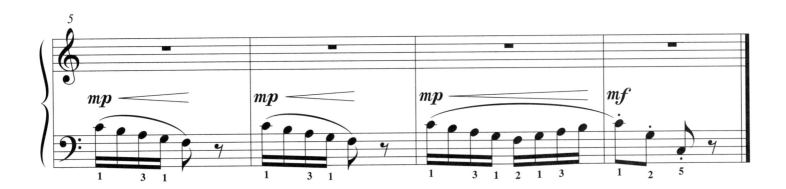

Transpose to: GM _____

AM _____

ETUDE

(Opus 82, No. 34)

Cornelius Gurlitt
(1820 -1901)

- Remember to play on the pads of your fingers for the best sound.
  Lift for the rests precisely to make the rhythm clear.

ETUDE

(Opus 117, No. 12)

Cornelius Gurlitt
(1820 -1901)

- Use weight transfer to play the five-finger and octave scale patterns, slightly
  dropping your wrists and forearms when playing with your thumbs on downbeats.

Etude in C

Study in Scales

Timothy Brown
(1959-   )

• Practice for a light, sparkly touch and sound.

Etude

(Opus 44, No. 8)

Albert Biehl
(1836-1899)

- Drop your arm weight on every first note of each five-finger pattern.
  Roll your wrist in the direction of the phrase and lift your wrist at the end of each phrase.

ETUDE

(Opus 101, No. 82)

Ferdinand Beyer
(1803-1863)

• Listen for complete evenness and no overlapping of notes in each scale.

ETUDE

(Opus 70, No. 33)

Hermann Berens
(1826-1880)

• Play the *staccato* notes clearly, pushing off the keys with your wrist and forearm.

UNIT 4 — SLURS AND PHRASING

As you continue to build your technique, refining the gesture needed for slurs and phrasing will be important to producing a musical effect. Each of the etudes included in this section emphasizes the use of the arm in two-or three-note slurs or in phrases. Rest your arm weight on the keys with fingers slightly curved, then roll your wrist slightly forward to bring the hand up and out of the keys. Imagine that you are measuring a wall with a measuring tape, and your forearm moves to follow the measuring tape up the wall. In the same way, the fingers follow the forearm, producing a gentle roll-off.

LAST RIDE ON A CAROUSEL

Suzanne Torkelson

Transpose to: DM _____

B♭M _____

ETUDE

(Opus 166, No. 12)

Henri Bertini
(1798-1876)

• Listen for a stronger first note and lighter second note in each two-note slur.

ETUDE

(Opus 108, No. 5)

Ludwig Schytte
(1848 -1909)

- Drop your weight into the keys on every strong beat and then roll forward and off for the second note of the two-note slur.

ETUDE NO. 5

from *The Pianist's First Music Making*

Tobias Matthay
(1858-1945)
Felix Swinstead
(1880-1959)

- Roll your wrist and forearm in the direction of the notes.
  Roll off at the end of each short phrase.

CARIBBEAN SUN

Valerie Roth Roubos
(1955-   )

- Push your forearm forward when playing every staccato note.
  Your wrist will naturally release in this manner.

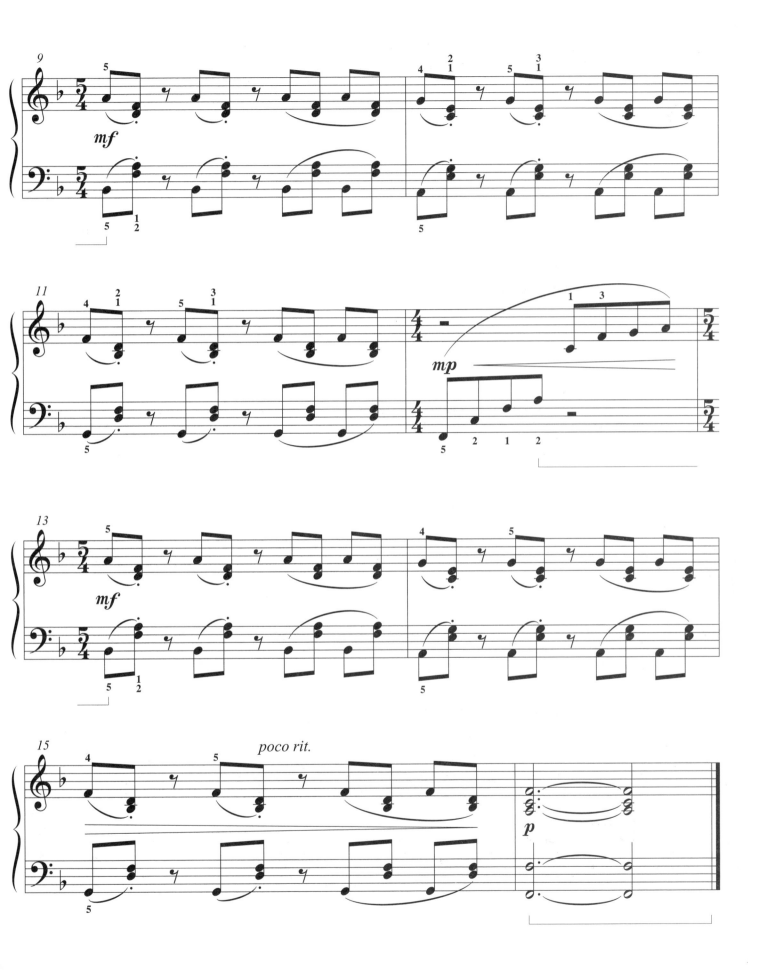

FJH2028

UNIT 5 — BROKEN CHORDS AND ALBERTI BASS

In this unit, you will find pieces that use broken chords as either accompaniment patterns or as melodic material. Remember that learning to play broken chords is often made easier by blocking them (play all notes of the chord together at the same time), then breaking them back apart when you have securely learned both hands. When you do know the notes, check that any zigzag motions of notes are played with an easy rotation of your hand and arm, as though you were trying to turn a light bulb in and out. Allow the weight of the hand to turn from side to side in an easy motion. For Alberti bass patterns, the rotation motion is small.

DUSK

Suzanne Torkelson

Slow and gentle

Play both hands one octave higher

Transpose to: B♭M _____

ETUDE

(Opus 108, No. 8)

Ludwig Schytte
(1848-1909)

- Practice the broken chord bass blocked (all notes together) with the R.H.
  Then practice the L.H. as written.

Impatience

(Opus 100, No. 23)

Alexandre Croisez
(1814-1886)

- Bring out the hand with the melody at all times.

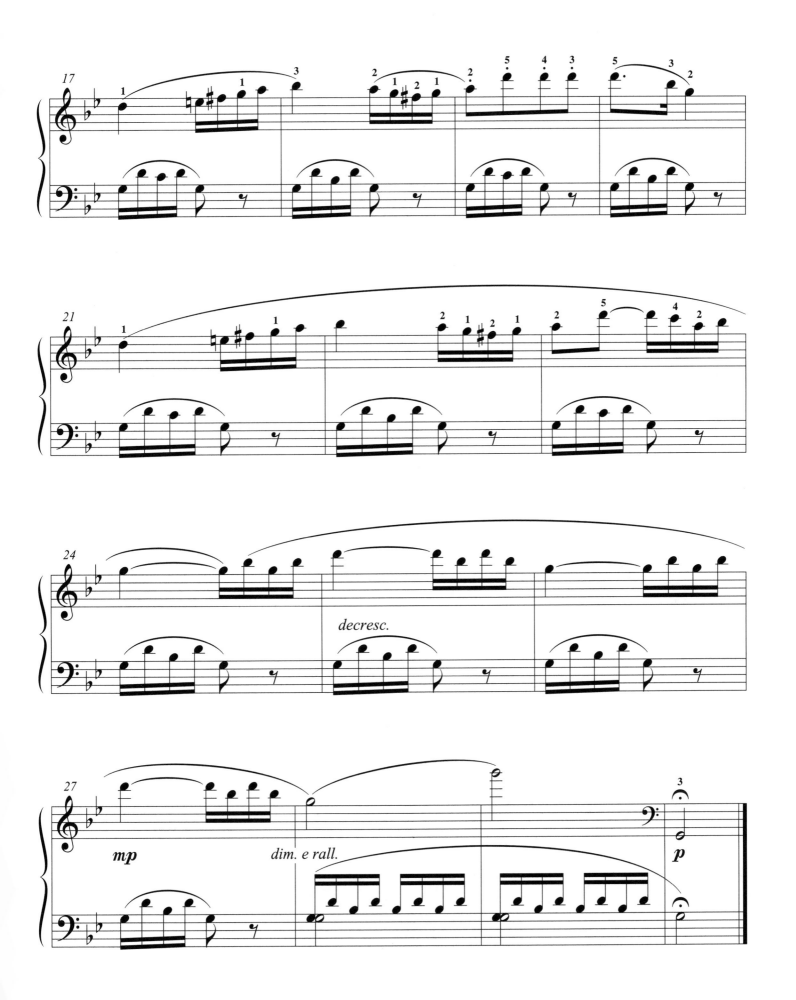

ETUDE NO. 58

from *Piano Method*

Johann Christian Bach
(1735-1782)
Francesco Pasquale Ricci
(1732-1817)

- Accent the downbeats slightly to keep the rhythm steady, and use a metronome.

UNIT 6 — DOUBLE NOTES

To play double notes precisely together, imagine that you wish to place a two-legged ladder against the wall. You know that if you tilt to one side or the other, the legs don't come down precisely together and the ladder isn't stable until both legs have equal weight on the floor. In the same way, when you play double notes, it is important to "place" the two fingers at precisely the same time, rather than landing with one slightly before the other. Shape each group in the air to be directly above them and keep the wrist flexible, with a small rebound from each drop. In this exercise, you can practice both thirds and sixths—play it fluently and quickly and have fun!

HAVING FUN!

Suzanne Torkelson

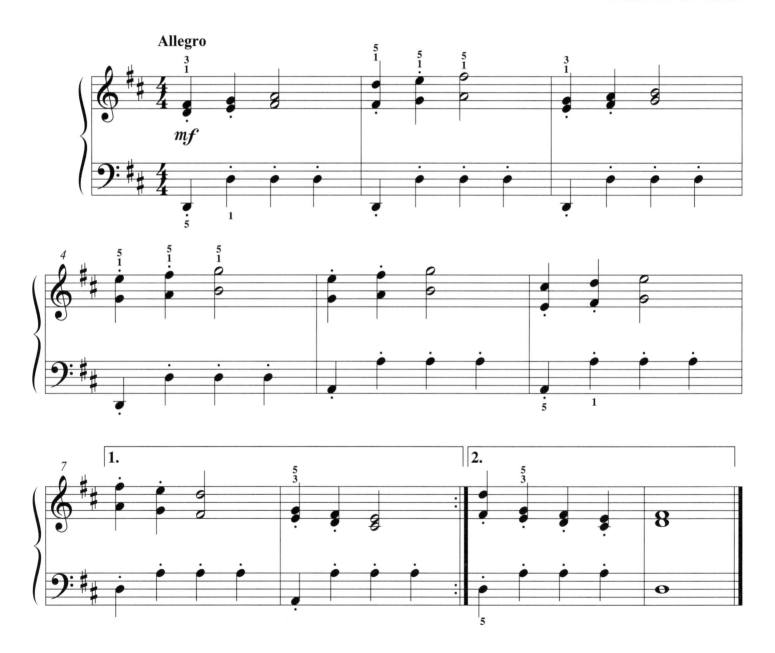

MINUET NO. 11

from *First Term at the Piano*

Béla Bartók
(1881-1945)

• Play with "spring," or bounce! Voice the top note of every interval of a 6th.

ETUDE

(Opus 139, No. 7)

Carl Czerny
(1791-1857)

- Play with a flexible wrist and bring out the top note in your R.H. Use a
  rebound staccato by throwing your hand into each blocked interval. As soon
  as the notes are played, rebound up and out of the keys, wrist first.

FOR PRACTICING THIRDS AND SIXTHS

Daniel Gottlob Türk
(1750-1813)

• Voice the top note of each 3rd or 6th.

UNIT 7 — REPEATED NOTES

When we play fast repeated notes on the piano, it is much easier to repeat the note with a different finger than to use the whole hand to make the down-up motion. Commonly, the fingers move sideways, as if you were lightly tapping one spot, but needed to use different fingers each time. As you play the following exercise, see how efficient you can be in getting the fingers that have played out of the way, shifting to the new one. It is fun to play them evenly and fast, and they sound very impressive to the listener when you get them up to speed!

TROTTING ALONG

Helen Marlais

Transpose to: DM _____

GM _____

ETUDE

(Opus 108, No. 10)

Ludwig Schytte
(1848-1909)

- "Kick off" the key every time you play your 5th finger.
  This motion will help propel you to the next notes.

ETUDE

(Opus 101, No. 90)

Ferdinand Beyer
(1803-1863)

- Play the eighth notes in the R.H. lightly and *staccato*. Drop into the longer notes, but feel as though you are moving through them rather than stopping on them.

PRANKS

Robert Schultz
(1948-   )

RINGELTANZ

(Round-dance)

(Opus 74, No. 17)

Cornelius Gurlitt
(1820 -1901)

- Play with a bounce in your wrists and you'll never tire!
- Shift the weight of your hand to the right for the sixteenth notes in m. 13-15.

51

FJH2028

ETUDE IN D MINOR

Timothy Brown
(1959-   )

• Play the repeated notes with a light arm. Drop into the key when playing with
your thumb, not to weigh down but to help give the feeling of forward direction.

ABOUT THE PIECES AND THE COMPOSERS

Unit 1 — Five-Finger Patterns and Extensions

Etude, *Opus 65, No. 7* by Albert Loeschhorn (1819-1905)
German composer and teacher Carl Albert Loeschhorn was born in Berlin and studied at the Royal Institute for Church Music there before he became a teacher of piano in 1851. He is best known for his numerous studies for the piano, which he most likely composed for his distinguished students. This etude uses stepwise patterns extended beyond the five-finger pattern, so practicing the right hand by blocking the groups of three notes leading to the thumb is a perfect way to learn the notes and the motions needed to play them fluently.

Etude, *Opus 17, No. 2* by Félix Le Couppey (1811-1887)
Le Couppey's set of etudes titled *The Alphabet* consists of 26 short pieces designated by the letters "A" to "Z," and deals with different techniques for playing the piano. To master the finger patterns of this etude, try blocking them and stopping at the end of each group to prepare the next. Notice when one hand has passagework, the other has longer note values, so you can focus on the hand that is more active.

Running Late by Valerie Roth Roubos (b. 1955)
This aptly titled etude is filled with running passages. The right hand begins with a running five-finger pattern, joined by the left hand in the second system. Perhaps the *staccato* repeated notes are the insistent honking in your driveway? When the meter changes to triple, begin softly and continue to crescendo until you reach the rest; then decrescendo to the final destination. Made it!

Tag, from *Children's Pieces, No. 8* by Soulima Stravinsky (1910-1994)
This etude was composed by the son of one of the greatest contemporary composers, Igor Stravinsky, and comes from a set of piano pieces intended to introduce young piano students to the sounds and colorful harmonies of 20th Century music. While one hand plays on white keys only, the other plays in another key, adding a very colorful flavor.

Allegro, *Opus 38, No. 19* by Hans Leo Hassler (1564-1612)
Hassler, a German organist and composer, studied in Italy and incorporated the style of Venice in his compositions. He is considered to be one of the most important German composers of all time, partly because he influenced many of the composers in the Baroque era. How many scale patterns can you find in this piece? Try marking them, especially noting when they are not a full eight-note pattern. Hassler found many opportunities to use scales here, giving you a chance to play them fluently within a piece.

Unit 2 — Triads and Inversions

Etude, *Opus 300, No. 75* by Louis Köhler (1820-1886)
Louis Köhler was a German composer, conductor, and piano teacher who studied in Vienna and worked in Königsberg, Germany. He was very successful as a piano teacher and composed many teaching etudes for his pupils. Although at first glance, this etude does not appear to have triads and inversions, it is a perfect example of how many pieces use notes that outline triads. If you block each measure silently, you will find that the notes are already under your fingers in triads and inversions. You might also try playing one hand with blocked chords and the other with individual notes; you will learn this piece very quickly!

Christmas Bells, *Opus 210, No. 25* by Louis Köhler (1820-1886)
In addition to performing and teaching, Köhler was also a music critic and contributor to important musical journals. He was well known to both Franz Liszt and Richard Wagner, two leading musicians of the Romantic era. Although this etude *sounds* very difficult, the left hand is a simple pattern of fifths that supports the triads and inversions of the right hand. As you learn the piece, focus on how each chord relates to the next one and on finding notes that stay the same or move stepwise. Imagine the sound of bells and use the pedal as marked to get a joyous, ringing effect!

The Return, *Opus 117, No. 24* by Cornelius Gurlitt (1820-1901)
This etude is from a collection by Gurlitt titled, *First Steps of the Young Pianist,* and follows a short, expressive piece called *The Departure.* The joy of seeing someone again is expressed here in the fast tempo, the rhythmic 6/8 meter, the variety in articulation, and the flowing broken triads. Learn each hand separately, blocking the notes silently into chords you recognize. When you have learned the patterns well, build your tempo until you reach the fast and happy character you might feel at seeing someone who has been away for a long time.

Etude No. 21, from *One Hundred Recreations* by Carl Czerny (1791-1857)
A brilliant teacher of many of the most famous pianists of the Romantic era, Czerny studied with Johann Nepomuk Hummel (a student of Mozart), Viennese court composer Antonio Salieri, and even Ludwig van Beethoven. His music for piano consists primarily of teaching pieces and etudes intended to develop piano technique. In this etude, the left hand plays broken chords as a smooth accompaniment to the singing melody. You may recognize the similarity of the melody to the American folk song *The Bear Went Over the Mountain,* which was originally an English and French tune.

Wind Master by Robert Schultz (b. 1948)
This study in broken chords for the left hand is both an etude and a dramatic solo work for the student pianist. Set in A minor, the eighth notes within the 6/8 meter provide a natural framework for the three-note broken chords that both ascend and descend by inversions of the tonic triad (A minor) as the work progresses. The mastering of this pattern of broken triads moving by inversions will provide a solid technical basis for the student to apply to similar chordal patterns throughout piano literature.

Unit 3 — Scale Preparation and Octave Scales

Etude, *Opus 82, No. 34* by Cornelius Gurlitt (1820-1901)
Gurlitt worked during the height of the Romantic era, when the Leipzig Conservatory in Germany was one of the most important music schools. He was a classmate of Carl Reinecke, whose father was a teacher at the conservatory. When the Schleswig-Holstein war broke out in 1849, Gurlitt became a military bandmaster. This tuneful etude will be good practice in playing five-finger patterns and scales. Observe the articulation and rests carefully to get the dance-like character of the triple meter.

Etude, *Opus 117, No. 12* by Cornelius Gurlitt (1820-1901)
After studying in Leipzig, Gurlitt moved to Copenhagen and studied piano, organ, and composition. He was acquainted with Robert Schumann and the Danish composer Niels W. Gade. Play the accompanying chords lightly detached to bring out the flow of the scale passages. Attention to the interesting contrast in dynamics also brings out the lively character of this etude.

Etude in C *(Study in Scales)* by Timothy Brown (b. 1959)
Although an entire scale is rare in this piece, you should note that all the right hand patterns outline scale segments. If you follow the fingering carefully, you will see how it is possible to compose an impressive melody with just the tones of a scale. Observe the articulation and tempo to create a cheerful character and fluent performance.

Etude, *Opus 44, No. 8* by Albert Biehl (1836-1899)
This etude is one in which you can enjoy the facility of five-finger patterns moving quickly around the piano. Although a few of the patterns include chromatic steps, most are five-note segments of major or minor scales that will help you learn the full scales later. When you can play this fluently, you will find this piece very impressive!

Etude, *Opus 101, No. 82* by Ferdinand Beyer (1803-1863)
As a classical musician, Ferdinand Beyer composed primarily teaching pieces, many of which he compiled into his *Elementary Instruction Book for the Pianoforte, Op. 101.* This etude, taken from that method, could be called "Follow the Leader" as the left hand echoes the scales of the right until they join together for a grand finish!

Etude, *Opus 70, No. 33* by Hermann Berens (1826-1880)
(Johann) Hermann Berens was born in Germany and first studied music with his father, a famous flute player. He was active as a music director at several theaters, and later moved to Sweden where he taught piano to nobility, including the queen of Sweden. This etude is a showcase of fluent scales in each hand and should be played with speed and clarity.

Unit 4 — Slurs and Phrasing

Etude, *Opus 166, No. 12* by Henri Bertini (1798-1876)
Henri Bertini was a child prodigy who moved from London to France and studied piano with his father and his brother, a student of Clementi. As a pianist, Bertini had a brilliant career and on one occasion, he gave a concert in Paris with the virtuoso Franz Liszt. Bertini was also well known as a teacher, and his method for piano and nearly 500 etudes have remained in the standard piano repertoire. This etude presents many opportunities to use the down-up motion of the two-note slur. The thirds are easy to play if you observe the fingering carefully; and the dotted rhythms of the last section outline four-note fingering groups.

Etude, *Opus 108, No. 5* by Ludwig Schytte (1848-1909)
A Danish composer, Schytte traveled to Germany to study with Franz Liszt. He later lived and taught in Vienna and Berlin. Although he was trained as a pharmacist, he composed a large number of teaching etudes as well as a few large works for piano and orchestra. In this etude, notice that the two-note slurs are played in alternating hands, but the chords are the same in both hands. It may help you to block this piece, playing the right and left hand together in blocked chords.

Etude No. 5, from *The Pianist's First Music Making* by Tobias Matthay (1858-1945) and Felix Swinstead (1880-1959)
This etude gives you practice in short groupings with roll off. Feel the division of the beat as triplets and notice that the last note is on the beat but often overlapped with an entry of the other hand. If you use the wrist and forearm to guide the fingers, you will be rolling off each hand in alternating groups, hearing beautiful shaping and feeling very graceful!

Caribbean Sun by Valerie Roth Roubos (b. 1955)
In addition to improving your two-note slurs, this etude will help you gain rhythmic mastery! You can learn the placement of your hands most easily by silently blocking each broken chord measure, then practice the roll off needed for the two-note slurs. When you have that mastered, count carefully to get the syncopation of Caribbean dances mixed with the 5/4 meter!

Unit 5 — Broken Chords and Alberti Bass

Etude, *Opus 108, No. 8* by Ludwig Schytte (1848-1909)
Practice the broken chords in the left hand as one-measure blocked chords to get your hand quickly over the notes and be able to focus on the movement of the right hand. When you can play it that way fluently, you will find that playing it as written will be a simple step. Play with clear differences in articulation and balance the melody against the broken chord accompaniment.

Impatience, *Opus 100, No. 23* by Alexandre Croisez (fl. 1814-1886)
What little is known about the life of Alexandre Croisez is that he was active as a composer in the 1850s, and he composed salon pieces to be performed in small home concerts. This etude is intended to be played in an agitated style, with the Alberti bass of the left hand adding a sense of impatience. Notice that you never play moving patterns in both hands at the same time, but rather alternate the hands that move in an agitated style.

Etude No. 58, from *Piano Method* by Johann Christian Bach (1735-1782) and Francesco Pasquale Ricci (1732-1817)
The eleventh and youngest son of Johann Sebastian Bach, Johann Christian was born when his father was already 50. He received his first music instruction from his father, then later from his famous brother, Carl Philipp Emanuel. The piano method of Johann Christian Bach and Pasquale Ricci taught specific techniques. The Alberti bass style of this etude is easiest to learn if you block the left hand while playing the right hand as written.

Unit 6 — Double Notes

Minuet No. 11, from *First Term at the Piano* by Béla Bartók (1881-1845)
This piece was taken from the piano method composed by Bartók and Sándor Reschofsky in 1913, which contained 18 pieces intended to teach piano in the earliest lessons. The melody of this etude is always accompanied by the interval of a sixth; notice that the only time the right hand plays other intervals is when the left hand has the melody.

Etude, *Opus 139, No. 7* by Carl Czerny (1791-1857)
Czerny was the first to use the word *"etude"* for a piece dedicated to one technical or musical concept. He composed over 800 collections of etudes for teaching such famous students as Beethoven's nephew and Franz Liszt. This melodious etude is best played detached with a free wrist, voicing the top note as the melody. Be sure to place your fingers on the keys before playing so that you will be accurate.

For Practicing Thirds and Sixths by Daniel Gottlob Türk (1750-1813)
Born in Germany the same year Johann Sebastian Bach died, Türk studied organ with his father and later with a student of Bach in Dresden, Germany. He became the director of music at Halle University in 1779, and a professor of music theory in 1809. This etude is from his *Klavierschüle,* a guide for teaching and learning the keyboard. When playing *legato* thirds, skips present a unique challenge. To get them to sound *legato,* you must play a perfect *legato* between the changing notes but lift and replay the repeated note that appears in both thirds. Stop and listen for the held *legato* and released note you must replay—once you hear it, you are ready to connect to the next one.

Unit 7 — Repeated Notes

Etude, *Opus 108, No. 10* by Ludwig Schytte (1848-1909)
As a pianist and teacher of piano, Ludwig Schytte composed many etudes for his pupils. This etude for repeated notes appears to have many different notes to learn, but a comparison of the measures reveals that there are just a few outlined chords, making it much easier to read and play. Observe the *staccato* and light touch for a cheerful effect.

Etude, *Opus 101, No. 90* by Ferdinand Beyer (1803-1863)
This delightful etude from the *Elementary Instruction Book for the Pianoforte* is a study on left-hand broken chords and right-hand double notes in the first and last sections. The middle section with its brilliant repeated notes and *marcato* double note melody in the left hand will be very impressive when you play it up to tempo.

Pranks by Robert Schultz (b. 1948)
A study that features 4-3-2-1 fingering for repeated note patterns in the right hand, while touching on a number of other important elements of keyboard technique, including a clear contrast between *legato* and *staccato* touch. *Pranks* is entirely on the white keys, achieving a whimsical contemporary harmonic flavor through the use of the dorian mode in D. The right-hand patterns alternate repeated notes and four note slurred groups that provide contrast, and encourage the student toward a successful execution of both types of elements. The crisp, quarter note motion of the left hand thirds provides a stable rhythmic basis and natural motor element for the study.

Ringeltanz (Round-dance), *Opus 74, No. 17* by Cornelius Gurlitt (1820-1901)
This etude is based on a German children's song in which they dance around a circle and sing about a bell ringing. At the end, notice the crescendo to the accented ring of the final chord. If you play the repeated notes with a light touch and agile bounce, you will produce even rhythms and the joyous character of the dance.

Etude in D Minor by Timothy Brown (b. 1959)
This characteristic etude was composed to explore the technique of playing repeated notes. Until you get comfortable with the right-hand patterns, block the left-hand chords, playing them softly but precisely on beat one and observe the fingering that makes the intervals easiest to find. Be sure to begin the last phrase softly so your final crescendo will be very exciting!